M&GN in Colour

VOLUME III

Edited by Dennis Greeno

Midland and Great Northern Joint Railway Society
Sheringham Station
Sheringham
Norfolk

The M&GN were joint owners, with the Great Eastern Railway, of two stretches of line in Norfolk and Suffolk. One was the route from North Walsham to Cromer *via* Mundesley whilst the other was between Yarmouth and Lowestoft. The construction of the latter was undertaken by the GE, with the M&GN providing its own connection from Yarmouth Beach over Breydon Bridge. Both lines constituted the 'Norfolk and Suffolk Joint Railway', and are considered part of the M&GN system for the purposes of this publication.

First published 2011
© The Midland and Great Northern Joint Railway Society

ISBN 978-0-904062-52-6

The Midland and Great Northern Joint Railway Society
Sheringham Station
Sheringham
Norfolk NR26 8RA

Design, photograph preparation and typeset by Dennis Greeno MCSD
The only costs incurred by the publisher were for copyright fees, printing and binding.

Printed in England.

TEXT AND CAPTIONS WRITTEN BY RICHARD ADDERSON, STEVE ALLEN AND DOUG WATTS

Acknowledgements

The circumstances that initiated this series were described on this page in Volume I and the three 'external' proofreaders, Mike Back, Mick Clark and Adrian Vaughan, have willingly taken on their task, yet again. Once again Philip Handford-Rice has supplied some information, on this occasion for the caption on page 20.

Thanks to Ron White, the former owner of Colour-Rail, and to Richard Adderson, John Clayson, the Great Eastern Railway Society, the M&GN Circle, and Brian Sullivan for the use of photographs in their collections.

Sources

Brooks P, *Weybourne,* Poppyland Publishing
Clark M J, *Midland and Great Northern Joint Railway*, Ian Allan ('Railway World' Special), 1990
Digby N, *A Guide to the Midland and Great Northern Joint Railway*, Ian Allan, 1993
Rhodes J, *The Midland & Great Northern Joint Railway*, Ian Allan, 1982
Wilkinson E, *Operation Norfolk*, Xpress Publishing, 2008
Wrottesley A J, *The Midland & Great Northern Joint Railway*, David & Charles, 1970
The District Controller's View: No. 12 The Midland and Great Northern Joint Railway, Xpress Publishing, 2009
M&GN Circle, *Bulletin*
M&GNJRS, *Joint Line*

INSIDE FRONT AND BACK COVERS: The M&GN was formed by the amalgamation of a number of small lines and brought under the control of the Midland and Great Northern companies in 1893. Relatively unaffected by the 1923 Grouping, the administration of the system was taken over by the LNER in 1936 and subsequently by British Railways. It consisted of 108 miles of single line and 74 miles of double track.

This map was originally published around 1900 in *Eastward Ho!* Colour prints on A3 paper are available from the M&GN shop at Weybourne and online at www.mandgn.co.uk

FRONT COVER: This undated shot, but believed to have been taken early on a Sunday morning in the spring of 1956, shows a typical mix, for the period, of ex-GER and new BR motive power on shed at Melton Constable. In the photograph are three 4MTs (the tender of one being just visible behind 62561), two J17s – the engine on the left facing the camera is 65509, J67/2 68536, and in centre foreground D16/3 62561.

The brick built shed in the centre was the Melton Constable running shed. The depot still stands in the industrial estate that now occupies the former works and station site.

PHOTOGRAPH: BRUCE CHAPMAN COLLECTION/ COLOUR-RAIL.COM BRE955

RIGHT: Ex-Great Central Railway D9 class 4-4-0 no. 6018 clears its cylinders as it departs from the LMS station at Melton Mowbray with a Birmingham to Yarmouth train in June 1946. This train would have diverged from the Leicester to Manton line at Saxby Junction and reached the M&GN metals at Little Bytham Junction. 6018 was one of 12 ex-Great Central D9s allocated to the M&GN section in 1937 and by 1946 it was one of the last four of the class on the system. The last of the four was withdrawn, or reallocated elsewhere, in March 1947.

THE LATE H N JAMES/COLOUR-RAIL.COM NE217

Little Bytham was where the Midland line from Saxby met end on with the M&GN from Bourne after crossing the Great Northern's east coast mainline on a lattice girder bridge. The Joint Line commenced here as, at one stage, it was envisaged that a curve from the east coast mainline would join the Midland line from Saxby. Little Bytham Junction was the point at which the Great Northern and Midland lines would have converged and thus an appropriate point for the M&GN to begin. In this photograph, Peterborough New England's 43085 approaches Little Bytham Junction with a Cromer to Birmingham train on the 7 January 1958. The first coach appears to be an ex-LMS Stanier Period III stock corridor brake first/composite. The locomotive is fairly clean, carries the later BR logo and is in unlined livery – which did nothing to improve the austere lines of these engines. The class was a precursor to the more aesthetically pleasing BR Standard 4MT.

The Great Northern Railway J22 class (classified J6 by the LNER)

This class was the final development of the GNR's 'Standard Goods' engines. These were its first goods locomotives to use superheating and piston valves. The first 15 emerged from Doncaster Works in 1911 (the year their designer, H G Ivatt, retired) and after minor modifications to the design a further 95 were built by H N Gresley up until 1922.

The J6s were based at many of the former GNR sheds from London up to west Yorkshire – with a number at Peterborough New England. These worked over the M&GN on freights and local passenger work right up to the 1959 closure of the syatem. The J6s were often referred to by enginemen as 'Knick-Knacks' due to the strange noise that they made when running with the steam shut-off. Withdrawals commenced in August 1955 with the last two going in June 1962. Unfortunately, none are preserved. This class was the last tangible link to M&GN motive power on the former M&GN metals. They were developed from the GNR J4s of which 12, from a batch of 25 built in 1900 by Dübs and Company, were delivered to the M&GN and classified as M&GN Da Class.

Ex-GNR J6 class 64172 and 4MT 43095 rest in the shed yard at Spalding early in the morning of 28 February 1959, the last day of passenger services over much of the M&GN system. Spalding had no locomotive allocation but the shed – at this time an outstation of Peterborough New England – was used as a stabling point until it closed in March 1960. Of interest is that the two classes to which these locomotives belong were designed by father and son – the J6s by Henry Arthur Ivatt for the GNR in 1911 and the 4MTs by his son Henry George Ivatt for the LMS in 1947.

Another photograph taken on 28 February 1959 of 64172 at Spalding. At this time the locomotive was a Peterborough New England engine, but upon closure of the M&GN it was moved to Boston shed. 64172 is on the 11.15 am local service to South Lynn – the service had started out as the 9.55 from Saxby, with this engine taking the train over here at Spalding. The rolling stock is composed of five ex-LMS Period III Stanier coaches. Of note is the large LNER blue enamel running-in board, a GNR water column and the GNR somersault bracket signal on the left. Signals near to a signal box were not usually fitted with wire-adjusters and having the arms pointing slightly upward was typical of this type, which somersaulted to off. There were three other somersault arms at Spalding, all pointing upwards at the end, and the Down starter at Gedney was just the same. The station had seven platforms (no. 4, a dock platform, was not used as such nor was it numbered) and usually the M&GN services to Sutton Bridge departed from platform 1. This train is in platform 6 because it is the only one accessible from the Bourne line. Spalding is still open today, though reduced to two platforms, on the Peterborough to Lincoln route.

An evocative rural scene at Tydd station on a crisp winter's day – 31 January 1959. The porter and signalman converse with the crew of South Lynn's 43144 as it stands at the head of a Peterborough North to Great Yarmouth train. The same train is shown in Volume 1, page 17, waiting to depart from Peterborough. Tydd was a remote station in the Fens to the south of Sutton Bridge in an area known as Tydd Gote on the north side of the North Level Main Drain. Originally built in 1866 with a single line, the passing loop and Down platform (pictured) were added in 1896 together with the M&GN signalbox. This signal box and that at Potter Heigham (*see* page 29), some 72 miles away, were built to the same 'Type 1' design. However, the Tydd signal box had an outside toilet at the top of its steps because of the lengthy walk to the one situated on the station. The criss-cross lattice fencing was a unique feature of the M&GN and was to be found at most stations on the M&GN system.

The same train has now reached Massingham on its journey east – in the distance the Up starter signal is 'off' to allow a train to pass in the opposite direction. In the foreground can be seen an example of the Whitaker tablet exchange apparatus for exchanging single line tablets without stopping. It was adopted by the M&GN in 1906 following a serious injury to a fireman here at Massingham. The footbridge is an original Eastern and Midlands Railway lattice girder type. This photograph shows all the stock in the train to be of Gresley design but apparently with no first class accommodation. The first coach is a wooden bodied corridor brake third, next comes a steel panelled corridor third, and lastly what appears to be a wooden bodied corridor third.

Melton Constable shed (BR shed code 32G)

The locomotive running shed at Melton was located on the south side of the station adjacent to the locomotive works. It opened in 1882 when the Eastern and Midland Railway first reached Melton. It was a three-road, 120 feet long, dead-end shed with panelled brick walls, a pitched slate roof, timber gables and four large smoke vents above each road. On the station side was a set of shear-legs (for lifting locomotives) and the shed's manually operated 47 feet diameter turntable. After 1945 the shed was in need of considerable improvements so in 1951 the BR Eastern Region modernised the shed (concurrent with the arrival of the first Ivatt 4MTs). It was rebuilt with glazed flush brick walls and a louvered concrete roof (*see* front cover photograph). Modernisation continued in 1953 when the turntable was replaced with a new 70 feet vacuum operated example. After closure the original was relocated to King's Cross in London in 1961, but its renaissance was short lived as steam finished there only three years later. The 1951 shed has fared much better, as it still stands (the front bricked up with roller doors providing access) and it is in use as a potato store.

This photograph, taken at Melton Constable at the same time as the front cover shot, shows BR Ivatt 4MT class 43151 glowing in the early morning light next to the 1951 shed. An unidentified sister locomotive can be seen in the background adjacent to the M&GN works drawing office building. 43151 was one of 12 of the Doncaster built class (43145–43156) allocated to Melton Constable from new in 1951. Under the thin layer of grime, the engine can be seen to be wearing the BR lined black livery and early BR crest. Note the recess mounted Whitaker tablet apparatus tucked away on the side of the tender. On closure of the M&GN 43151 was transferred to Stratford in east London and was withdrawn from Crewe South in December 1967.

BRUCE CHAPMAN COLLECTION/COLOUR-RAIL.COM BRE1380

Adjacent to 43151, in the previous photograph, is ex-GER J17 class 65586. As with 43151, it has a Whitaker tablet apparatus attached to the tender. In this instance it has been left in the operating position, rather than folded away, but as it protruded some ten inches it could easily get in the way! At this time 65586 was based at Yarmouth Beach depot, one of six allocated to the M&GN in the 1940s to replace life expired ex-M&GN classes. Fitted with steam heat and vacuum brakes, they were used in a mixed traffic capacity on the system. They were often called 'Sweedie 4s' by M&GN enginemen, *see* page 6 of Volume II.

The photographer's 'catch' at Melton Constable that Sunday morning also included Norwich Thorpe based D16/3 'Super Claud' 62561 – it is seen here, still with some steam emanating from the valves, outside the new running shed. Despite several rebuildings, the locomotive still retains its distinctive GER smokebox door ring. This variant has the straight 'cut away' footplating and round topped Gresley boiler. 62561 was withdrawn at Melton in February 1958 and scrapped at Stratford works just two months later. The tall, brick chimney was for the works foundry.

GER 'Claud Hamilton' D16/3 4-4-0

The lineage of the D16/3s originated with Holden's GER no. 1900, built in 1900 and named *Claud Hamilton*. Between 1900 and 1923, 120 engines were built by the GER and LNER to the same basic design, though with continual improvements made over the years. The last batch of ten new locomotives was classified D16 and they were nicknamed 'Super Clauds'. From 1915 onwards many of the earlier examples were rebuilt to match their newer brethren. In 1933 a major change was made to the design with the introduction of Gresley round-topped boilers and improved valves – they were classified D16/3. By 1949, when the rebuilding programme finished, the D16/3s totalled 104 examples.

In their time, the 'Clauds' were the largest and most powerful express locomotives on the GER and so were put to work on the principal express services. But by the late 1940s several were allocated to the M&GN section to replace older 4-4-0s that had been drafted in to supersede M&GN 4-4-0s.

Withdrawals started in 1955 with the last, 62613 (*see* page 27 of Volume I), being withdrawn from March shed in November 1960.

Tucked behind 62561 was ex-GER 0-6-0 68536, a member of the J67/2 class. The J67/2s were rebuilds of the earlier J69s introduced by James Holden in the 1890s as the R24 class. 68536 was built in April 1892 and withdrawn in February 1958. At first glance it looks as though the shunter is sporting an express passenger headcode, but it was one of two Yard and Works pilots, neither of whom hardly ever ventured beyond Melton whilst allocated there. Much more likely is one lamp shows a white light, the other a red – the station pilot headcode. It is interesting to note the photographs on this, the preceeding three pages and the front cover show locomotives with their lamps left *in situ*. At one time these were in short supply and enginemen disposing a locomotive would have to return the lamps to the stores, if only for topping up with paraffin and trimming of the wick. Drivers and firemen signing on would collect the necessary lamps from the stores together with a sponge, cloths and so on.

For five years after the main closure passenger trains continued to run between Sheringham and Melton Constable – the former hub of the M&GN system lingered on as a branch line terminus. Despite this reduction in services, the view eastward along the platform was remarkably unchanged during the final period. The view, looking west, from the signal in the distance was shown on page 36 of Volume I. Melton East signal box continued to control the movements of the passenger trains, which arrived at the northern face of the island platform, shunted forward and then departed from the south face. Even the junction signals for the Yarmouth and Norwich lines, by now lifted and serving as a headshunt respectively, remained in place. The signals on the left are of the somersault pattern, whilst those to the right, partially hidden by the roof of the signalbox, are of the more modern upper quadrant design. On the extreme left is a modern electric light post, one of a series installed along the full length of the platform after the 1959 closures. The expenditure on this was the subject of much adverse comment, as the DMUs then forming the passenger trains occupied a very small proportion of the platform's length.

Signals

Although Midland Railway lower quadrant signals (*see* page 25 of Volume I) were found on some M&GN lines, more characteristic of the M&GN scene was the somersault signal derived from the Great Northern pattern and showing all clear in a near vertical position, as on page 20. The signal arms were often attached to a concrete signal post constructed at Melton works. Towards the end of the line's life these somersault signals, and many lower quadrant signals, were being replaced by upper quadrant signals (*see* page 16). Indeed, one of the signalling staff associated with the reclamation of signalling equipment noted he was taking down signals he had erected only a few years previously.

Some parts of the M&GN also had installed some early versions of colour light signalling such as at South Lynn (*see* page 20 of Volume II), Melton East and Clay Lake, Spalding, and – much later in 1950 – at Murrow where they protected the crossing on the level of the M&GN and the joint Great Eastern and Great Northern line to the north.

Another of the electric lights can be seen on the wall to the left, which encloses the staircase providing public access to the island platform. This photograph was taken on the final day of services, 4 April 1964. Even at this late date, there were plenty of details to savour, such as the weighing machine and the brazier. The latter stands on the private platform to the right, which was provided for the use of the local landowner, Lord Hastings. Careful study of the spandrels on both platforms shows the initials 'CNR' (Central Norfolk Railway), a company that was associated with an early, but unsuccessful, attempt to build the rail link between Melton and North Walsham. The train is the 2.56 pm to Norwich Thorpe, which departed soon afterwards with a valedictory fusillade of detonators exploding beneath its wheels.

Diesel services

Diesel multiple units became a familiar sight at Melton Constable from September 1957, when they replaced steam traction on most local workings on the Norwich and Cromer lines. These trains offered only second class accommodation and the timetables for the two branches emphasised this fact.

The units did not just shuttle back and forth on their respective lines, but included various through workings between Norwich City and Sheringham and Cromer, and sometimes on to Norwich Thorpe. In addition, two of the units made trips between Melton and Fakenham on weekdays. The weekday 4.15 pm departure from Fakenham was essentially a school train taking home passengers from Fakenham Grammar School, whereas the 6.31 arrival was a very useful service from Norwich City to Fakenham. These were the only regular DMU workings on any part of the M&GN other than the Norwich and Cromer branches.

After the 1959 closure, passenger trains continued to reach Melton from the Cromer direction. These were mainly through trains from Norwich Thorpe, but there were a few short distance services serving Melton to and from either Cromer or Sheringham. Diesel multiple units all but monopolised these post-1959 trains, and gradually the originals, built by Metro Cammell, were joined by the similar Derby lightweight units. These two types, working on sometimes quite complex diagrams, continued to operate the line until the end of services on the Sheringham to Melton Constable section on 4 April 1964. By then, all the trains serving Melton Constable ran to or from Norwich Thorpe, with the exception of one early morning trip from Sheringham to Melton and return. The Sheringham to Cromer section is the only part of the M&GN to retain passenger services between the two towns and Norwich.

BERNARD WALSH/GREAT EASTERN RAILWAY SOCIETY

Here is the ornate signal box at Roughton Road Junction, photographed from the front seat of a diesel unit during the early 1960s. The trackbed of the Norfolk and Suffolk Joint line to Mundesley, closed in 1953, is clearly defined to the left of the box, while there is evidence of the former double track formation. Boarded up windows show that the building is no longer in use – it was closed in June 1961 and demolished a few years later. Trains on the Bittern Line continue to run over this curved section of track, which originally provided a link between the N&SJ and the Great Eastern line to Norwich. The location is just to the east of the current Roughton Road station, but today the site of the junction is almost unrecognisable .

This is a pre-preservation view of Weybourne station just six months before BR closed the line to passenger services. A Metropolitan Cammell Lightweight DMU (a precursor to similar looking Class 101) arrives with the 2.12 pm Norwich Thorpe to Melton Constable on the 17 October 1963. By this date the Up line and loop was already out of use, having closed in June 1961. Despite the remoteness of the station from Weybourne village (a mile away) there are prospective passengers waiting on the platform. The station appears run down with faded paintwork and with sections of the canopy roof missing. A single wagon lies in the yard adjacent to the loading dock. After closure the flat bottomed track was quickly lifted for reuse by BR and the Up platform waiting shelter and signalbox demolished.

There was no station here until 1900 when this one was built to serve a grand hotel 'Weybourne Springs' just adjacent to the line. Whilst the station survived and catered for many thousands of troops visiting the nearby army camp in the Second World War, the hotel started to suffer from settlement, being built on sandy ground, and was eventually demolished in 1939 both as a dangerous structure and because it provided a conspicuous landmark for incoming enemy aircraft.

Another pre-preservation view, this time of Sheringham East signalbox and crossing on the 29 May 1965. A Metro Cammell Lightweight unit (with yellow panel and red skirt rather than the speed whiskers seen in the previous photograph) sets off past an M&GN somersault signal for Cromer and Norwich. At this date trains from Cromer Beach terminated in the M&GN station at Sheringham, the Up platform of which was taken out of use on 2 January 1965 only to be brought back into operation on 23 June, just under a month after this photograph was taken. As an economy measure to permit the closure of the signalbox and level crossing, BR built a new halt on the east side of Station Road. The old station closed and the new halt opened on 2 January 1967. The crossing remained intact for a few more years permitting transfer of stock onto the newly formed North Norfolk Railway. By the early 1970s a road improvement scheme swept away the crossing and cattledock, whilst the signalbox with its wheel for working the gates was relocated onto platform 2 of the preserved station.

CEDRIC A CLAYSON

Another view of Sheringham level crossing. It is seen here in the early 1960s from a departing DMU on the Down line to Cromer – the driver receives the single line token in its hooped leather pouch from the Sheringham East signalman, believed to be Arthur Bailey. The line became single just beyond Smiths shoe repair shop, the facing points being protected by the Up home signal, a somersault arm. The area beyond the crossing is where British Rail built the new halt – opened in January 1967 – after the M&GN station and crossing were closed. This level crossing was reinstated early in 2010, reconnecting the North Norfolk Railway with the national network for the first time in 40 years.

Holiday camps

The railways stimulated the development or expansion of holiday towns – in Volume II the important role of the M&GN in the growth of Sheringham was noted. Major developments may have been expected at Caister as the Grand Hotel at Sheringham was constructed by the Sheringham and Caister Hotel Company. However, holiday patterns began to change and by 1939 the 12 holiday camps established between Corton and Hemsby were perhaps the largest cluster on the English coast. These developments were free from town planning constraints – legislation came into force in 1947 and restricted developments along the coastline.

One of the earliest was Caister (developed by J Fletcher Dodd) which began operations in 1906 with visitors staying in tents, which were soon replaced by chalets, and by 1949 it covered 90 acres and accommodated 800 people per week. The camp claimed to be the oldest in the UK and, of relevance to the M&GN, the only pre-war camp with its own railway station – it survives today as Caister Holiday Village. Caister acted as an exemplar for further development. Camps were set up either as small scale family ventures such as Pa Potter at Hemsby (later transferred to Hopton) or by workers' organisations such as the Rogerson Hall Camp at Corton, established by the Workers Travel Association (linked with the Co-operative movement). A late addition was Gorleston holiday camp that opened in 1937 but it is now the site of a housing estate (*see* page 15 of Volume I). Mundesley had its own camp, opened in 1935, and was the only one close to the north Norfolk section of the N&SJ.

The 1950s and 1960s have been described as the golden age of the holiday camps. Fortuitously the M&GN, and its extension the Norfolk and Suffolk Joint, ran through these major new additions to the English seaside scene.

43143 of Melton Constable passes Caister Camp Halt (three quarters of a mile north of Caister on Sea) with a holiday Saturday express for Yarmouth on 13 July 1957. Caister Holiday Camp had its own halt opened in 1933 (*see* page 14 of Volume II). It was one of a series of halts between Potter Heigham and Yarmouth opened to build on the growing holiday industry and to supplement the coastal stations of Caister and Hemsby. The holidaymakers sitting on the verandah are probably enjoying a cup of tea, purchased in the Holiday Cafe – the cafe also acted as reception for guests arriving by train. However, none of the Saturday holiday trains from the Midlands stopped at Caister Camp Halt, the only express service to do so was the 'Holiday Camps Express' from Liverpool Street (*see* page 27 and page 9 of Volume I). Locomotive, coaching stock and time of day suggest this is the 9.21 am fast from Peterborough to Yarmouth. This service was unusual in two ways. It seems to have been the only summer Saturday express from South Lynn to Yarmouth diagrammed regularly for Melton locomotives and it was the only fast service to originate from the Peterborough line. Surprisingly, there was no balancing fast return working. This service took 3 hours 54 minutes for the 110 miles compared with between 4 hours 9 minutes and 4 hours 31 minutes for the Saturday stopping services to Yarmouth.

With the Caister Up home signal 'off', that is in the 'all clear' position, the summer Saturday service from Yarmouth to Derby is passing non-stop through Caister on Sea's single platform on 20 July 1957. The service was the 9.30 am departure from Yarmouth Beach and was scheduled to arrive at journey's end, Derby, at 3.55 pm. This is an unusual working for 62517, a D16/3 class locomotive, as the longer, heavier holiday trains were usually hauled by either the new Ivatt 4MT locomotives or the older GER B12s – both classes were more powerful than the D16/3s. It is probable that a shortage of motive power led Yarmouth shed to use the 62517 instead of a B12. There was only a single goods siding, the end of which appears here next to Beach Road level crossing, which emphasises that Caister was predominantly a passenger station with limited demand for freight facilities.

LNER B12 4-6-0s

Designed by Stephen Holden, the GER s69 class (which became LNER B12) was a powerful inside cylindered 4-6-0 layout – between 1911 and 1920 the GER built 70 of these locomotives. In 1928 the LNER was in urgent need of extra express passenger engines for its Great Eastern section so, as a stop gap, a further ten B12s were ordered from Beyer Peacock. Modernisation of the class began in 1932 and 44 of the GER types and the ten LNER locomotives were rebuilt with larger round topped boilers and were classified B12/3. Many of the unrebuilt engines ended their days in Scotland. During the Second World War a number of the class were requisitioned to haul military ambulance trains in south-west England after D-Day. In 1948 six B12/3s were allocated to South Lynn and Yarmouth Beach sheds to work the heavy 'Leicesters' (*see page 21 of Volume II*). Withdrawals of the B12/3s commenced in 1947, with many going on the completion of the Southend electrification in 1956. After 1959, 61572 was the sole surviving example and became a depot mascot at Norwich Thorpe until withdrawn in May 1961. It now operates on the North Norfolk Railway (*see page 17 of Volume II*).

THE LATE E ALGER/COLOUR-RAIL.COM BRE2171

The photographer, standing on the Jellicoe Road overbridge, captures a view of 61540 nearing Yarmouth on the afternoon of 6 July 1957 with a summer Saturday service from the Midlands. The train is passing Yarmouth racecourse which is just out of the picture to the left. The extensive area of caravans beside the track highlights the importance of the holiday trade to this part of Norfolk. The locomotive would have worked out to South Lynn in the morning before returning to its home shed of Yarmouth in the afternoon.

ERIC FRY/COLOUR-RAIL.COM BRE951

A freight composed of five vans next to the engine, as was normal practice, and a considerable number of mineral wagons leaves Yarmouth Beach at 3.40 pm with 43107 of South Lynn in charge. The view could be typical of any day on the M&GN in the 1950s as the slot was timetabled for a service to Saxby. However, as this photograph was taken on 28 February 1959, 43107 is probably moving the remaining stock from Yarmouth Beach yard. To the rear of the train two goods sheds can just be seen whilst the engine shed is out of shot away to the left. The close proximity to the railway of the housing on Wellesley Road caused problems arising from noise and smoke for both residents and M&GN staff. 43107 was sent to Boston when the M&GN closed and was amongst the earliest to be withdrawn as one of a batch of four in December 1963.

Freight in the 1950s

An idea on the importance of freight is provided by the number of services in both directions between Melton and South Lynn in the winter of 1957–8. On Mondays to Fridays 11 passenger trains a day (nine stoppers and two fast) were accompanied by no less than 14 freight services (including a parcels train).

Freight carryings were dominated by agricultural produce and the flow was predominantly outwards from the M&GN area. Inward goods tended to be general merchandise and coal. The latter was mostly domestic though there was also a regular daily trainload from the Midlands to the gasworks by Norwich City station. Agricultural traffic was highly seasonal, especially in the Fens. There the patterns were very similar to that in the post 1959 period (*see* page 26 of Volume I) with daily outward flows of perishable, horticultural produce beginning with spring flowers, then soft fruits, later vegetables and then autumn fruit such as apple and pears. Autumn also saw the movement of sugar beet to factories in Spalding and King's Lynn and in the east *via* the link with the Great Eastern to Cantley.

The summer Saturday through train from the East Midlands has arrived at Gorleston on Sea on 31 August 1957. It was scheduled to leave Derby at 9.55 am, Leicester at 10.52 and was due to reach Gorleston at 3.34 pm. Now, after a long cross country journey *via* Stamford, Peterborough, Ely and Norwich, some of the passengers have at last arrived at their holiday destination, only to find the weather is not very summery – no wonder the two little girls in their raincoats look a little glum. Until 1953 this train ran over the M&GN main line, reversing at Yarmouth Beach to reach its destination.

Whilst the Saturday holiday trains provided the main interest for the railway enthusiasts at the time, the all year round stopping trains serving all the stations between Yarmouth and Lowestoft attracted less attention. Here is one of these locals, the 3.26 pm from Yarmouth, pausing for custom at Hopton on 13 October 1956. The locomotive is C12 class 4-4-2T 67366, built to a Great Northern Railway design dating back to 1898. A few of these engines worked in East Anglia during the 1950s and this one was based at Yarmouth South Town shed from April 1955 until it was withdrawn some three years later. Other engines of the class were used on the M&GN in the far west of Norfolk, operating the pull-push trains between King's Lynn and South Lynn.

Here is the 3.26 pm train from Yarmouth about a year later, leaving Hopton on 2 August 1957. The station can be seen round the curve in the distance, partially obscured by the smoke from the locomotive, N7 class 69706. The N7s were built specifically for operating suburban trains out of Liverpool Street and some found their way out into the country areas when the suburban services were electrified. Oddly, 69706 went the other way, working from Norwich and Lowestoft throughout the 1950s, before being allocated to Stratford in September 1959 for the last year or so of its existence. As with some of the C12 class on the previous page, the N7s were also to be found on the King's Lynn to South Lynn services. Behind the train, the transition from embankment to cutting contradicts the popular belief that East Anglia is flat.

The LNER L1 class 2-6-4Ts

The LNER had not favoured this wheel arrangement following the Sevenoaks crash on the Southern in 1927, so it was not until May 1945 that the prototype L1 2-6-4T no. 9000 was introduced by Edward Thompson. This was to be the passenger tank design for the LNER and incorporated standard components including B1 cylinders and the bogie from A1 class rebuilds. Although an order for 30 was placed in 1944, 9000 was the only example in service until after nationalisation in 1948. The remaining 99 were built between 1948 and 1950. The class was primarily intended for suburban and stopping passenger services, and the locomotives were mostly based in larger cities where they ousted older types such as ex-GER F5s and F6s, ex-GNR C12s, and ex-NER G5s. A small number were also allocated to Ipswich, Norwich and Lowestoft. It is the engines at the latter shed (in 1955 they were 67704, 67714 and 67717) that ventured onto the Norfolk and Suffolk Joint line. The L1s had a fairly undistinguished career and the East Anglian examples had migrated to Stratford by 1960. With rapid dieselisation they were soon surplus to requirements the last being withdrawn in 1962.

Early in the season L1 class 2-6-4T 67704 arrives at Corton station on 1 June 1957. The first coach carries a 'Holiday Camp Express' roofboard, which identifies it as one of the Saturday through trains from Liverpool Street to Gorleston. 67704 entered service in early 1948 and was withdrawn from Stratford in November 1960.

'Holiday Camps Express'

As life returned to some degree of normality after the Second World War, workers were able to take advantage of the paid holidays which had only recently become their legal right. As noted on page 21, seaside holiday camps became increasingly popular and British Railways capitalised on this popularity by running Saturday trains from Liverpool Street specifically to serve the camps in the Corton, Hopton and Gorleston areas. By 1952, and to 1957, there were three morning trains from Liverpool Street to Gorleston, leaving at 8.05, 10.15, 11.12 am and one afternoon service at 3 pm. Journey times varied between 3 hours 3 minutes and 3 hours 44 minutes. They were specified in the timetables as 'Holiday Camps Express', and many of them carried roofboards on the carriages bearing the 'Holiday Camps Express' name. The summer of 1958 was the last in which the 'Holiday Camps Express' title was officially used. In the summer of 1959 there were still three Gorleston to Liverpool Street trains on Saturdays, but they were no longer distinguished with a title in the timetable. Further north, on the M&GN proper, another 'Holiday Camps Express' served the camp at Caister during the same summers. It, too, was so described in the timetables and carried roof boards to distinguish it from lesser trains. The 1952 timing was typical – leaving Liverpool Street at 10.50 am, it ran *via* Ely, the Wensum curve to avoid Norwich, and on to North Walsham, where it reversed and ran south over the M&GN to let passengers off at Hemsby, Caister Camp Halt and Caister on Sea. It was scheduled to arrive there at 3.21 pm. In the opposite direction, the train left Caister at 10.38 am and deposited the homeward bound holidaymakers at Liverpool Street some 4 hours and 50 minutes later. It last ran in the summer of 1958.

THE LATE E ALGER/COLOUR-RAIL.COM

A few weeks later a 'Holiday Camp Express' waits to leave Corton on 6 July 1957. The guard looks back along the train to ensure that all the doors are closed, and that it will be safe for him to wave his green flag to authorise the driver of 62571 to set out on the short run to the next station, Hopton. A small girl and her mother are looking out of the window, eager to get to their holiday destination. Whether it is Gorleston or Hopton, they have not long to wait now.

Demolition

Work dismantling the railway began on the Monday morning after closure. Some people say this was the act of a vindictive railway management who wanted to ensure there was no chance of the line being re-opened. The truth is probably less emotive – a pool of labour was available whose redundancy could be deferred and there was little point in leaving valuable assets to deteriorate when they could be used elsewhere. The turntable at Melton, for example, was taken away for further use at King's Cross. On the main line, demolition work started at Sutton Bridge working eastwards to South Lynn, at East Rudham working eastwards to Melton Contable. and at Yarmouth Beach working back to Melton. On the latter two sections at least trains were run to collect stores and materials from the stations, before track lifting began. Rail mounted steam cranes were used on the double track sections, but photographs suggest that much of the work on the route north from Yarmouth was done by a road crane – presumably there was insufficient space to manoeuvre a rail crane on the single track. Most, if not all, of the track sections from the Yarmouth to East Rudham section were taken away by rail to the disused station at Cromer High where the material was sorted and reusable components were identified. Progress was rapid and less than a month after closure, the lines had been lifted between East Rudham and Raynham Park. By the summer of 1960, all track on the totally closed sections in Norfolk had been removed.

COLOUR-RAIL.COM

In October 1959 a demolition train, headed by J39 class 0-6-0 64761, makes its way along the low embankment near Potter Heigham Bridge Halt. Demolition began immediately after closure and indeed, on the final day of operation, bogie bolsters (long, low wagons for carrying track panels) were already in the sidings at Yarmouth and Melton Constable ready for the process of reclamation of track and fittings which began 48 hours later.

On the same day 64761 stands in the platform at Potter Heigham. The low autumn sun brings out the colours of the signal box, while piles of redundant equipment litter the surrounding platform. Perhaps surprisingly, the signal box still retains its name board after eight months of abandonment. However, the railway collector's market was still in its infancy in those days and in 1959 such things were not as highly prized as they are today. The similarity of this signal box to that at Tydd (page 7) is clear.

Whilst most of the M&GN closed to passengers at the end of February 1959, many sections remained open for goods traffic. On the 27 May 1961 BR British Thompson Houston Type 1 Bo-Bo (later Class 15) D8206 pulls away from Whitwell and Reepham on an Up freight formed of BR 'Palvans' (pallet vans) whilst a Norwich bound freight sits in the Down platform. The BTH Class 15 was a BR pilot scheme freight design that was beset with problems with the Paxman engine and most were withdrawn by 1971, though four were retained for electric train heating (ETH) duties. D8233, one of the ETH units, has survived into preservation at the East Lancashire Railway. Class 15s were not common on the M&GN, this being a Norwich Thorpe based example. The footbridge was a Norfolk and Suffolk Joint Railway type, moved here in 1930 from Felbrigg Woods to replace an earlier wooden version. The signalbox visible through the footbridge is an Eastern and Midlands example, *see* also page 26 of Volume II. The Up starting signal was a replacement upper quadrant arm on a M&GN concrete post. Note the height the lampman had to climb to reach the lamp and the lack of a 'safety hoop' at the top.

With the factory complex to the right of the train, Brush type 2 no. 5629 stands at the Anglian Concrete Products works, Lenwade, with a train of concrete beams on 26 June 1970. The first trainloads of such items had run in the 1950s and this traffic continued until the Lenwade line closed. The last service train ran in September 1981 and it was officially closed on 16 June 1983. Earlier in the century, the M&GN had been a pioneer in the use of concrete for items such as signal posts, fencing, mileposts, platform walls and station nameboards, establishing in the process a reputation for this work. It is therefore an interesting quirk of history that the same material enabled a short section of the system to remain open for 23 years after the main closure.

D2018 stands in the goods yard at Norwich City on 4 June 1968. There are enough wagons in the extensive yards to justify the provision of a station shunter, which had to make the long journey back to Norwich Thorpe *via* Themelthorpe whenever it required attention. A party of members of the Norfolk Railway Society, armed with permits to travel on the brake van of the morning goods, has gathered to await their train. The shunter was built at Swindon, entered service at Hitchin in April 1958, was withdrawn from Norwich Crown Point in November 1975 and has been preserved in East Anglia at Mangapps Farm Railway.